WARPED

A Writer's Journey

By: Conor Keating

Warped
© 2025 Conor Keating
ISBN 9781966337270
Library of Congress control number: 2025922979

Cover art © 2025, Jeff Otto
Photography/Art © 2025, Paul Deardorff, Solar Dunn, Conor Keating, Sean Keating,
Lisa Sarff, Robin Sarff

First Edition 2025

Printed in the United States of America

Edited by Cherice Cameron
Cover design by: Jim Dodson
Layout design by: Erica Castro

The poems is this book are dedicated to –

Brian, Sean, Karen, Paul and Monica

Acknowledgments

I would like to acknowledge The University of Idaho English Department where I completed my Bachelors in creative writing in 2008, specifically professors Robert Wrigley, Monica Mankin, Joy Passanante, and Alexandra Teague who helped workshop several of these poems in their infancy as well as taught me poetic theory. I also want to thank Community Literature Initiative Season 12 for helping me finish this work.

Warped: A Writer's Journey

Table of Contents

Part IV. Love

Part V. After

Part I. Beginnings

Lightning the Universe by: Sean Keating

The Front Street Poets

In her madness a girl named Molly, who loved the written verse,
Called out to the poets in the streets to share,
To dangle in man's verbal dignity, once more
In the café.

Art rips across the skies
And the Front Street poets answer,
The call to speak with a voice,
Drifting down the crosswalk of Main Street.

Homeless, loud, stuffy and robust,
Hypnotic in verse, they come
Skating in on grocery carts,
Bicycles equipped with bathtubs,
Imagination, sonnets,
With no thing you have ever seen.

With French wine
Pouring the color red they come,
In sips against their lips
As they burst upon the front door

With cowboy hats, cigarettes, profound statements
From Aristotle, to napkins professing love of Cheddar Gouda
Greeting man's magical wonderful love of Wisconsin, if you please.
Irish dandies among the voices, mingled, sharing past perceptions
Mimicking Yeats and Keats in form, as they try to impress the women
Poet ladies who bring humor to their words,
Explaining the reasons why they made their boyfriend change the
Sheets after sexual fragrant nakedness in that summer spent in New York

That summer of beat box voices visiting from L.A, picking up the rhythm
In the Bronx-speak of sharp Ginsberg's prose, with practice,
Making us think about prostitution in America, sounds of
Hip-hop vice city beats
Voices in the coffee hall
They will blast a crowd
In the room of street personas come together

To paint on the door
"Poets Welcome Open Mic"
"Red Carpet Ready for the Front Street Poets, Welcome!
Drink Your Coffee, Sip Your Slurps, and Take It In!"

'Cause this is just beginning.

Watching Shakespeare
(For James Earl Jones)

I smell the cold crisp sulfur from the stage torches
The Old Man now gone
Sits upon his mark to play the mighty Lear
A booming Mississippi crafted performance in America

If only I had played
The Fool on stage gently in that moment
Before he was Vader
Or Mufasa, or a writer of baseball

This artist who is Lear in Central Park
Contemplating the words of The Bard

I wonder where James is now
Sleep well, my good King

Ants Capturing a Watermelon

The drips of seeds
Dissect so innocently
The ground of youth
Where a rotting discarded corpse
Lies naked in the grass.
Trophies from the battle
Delicately rise in hand,
Their lush richness carried
Away with pride, as it will feed
The homeland in the cold breath of winter,
Yet a few of the unfortunate souls never see
Home again.

Ancient samurai are faced with the good
And honorable death
Worthy of an emperor,
As legs are broken and organs burst
At the mercy of a child's hand
That thinks not of death
But only of trying to savor
One last moment of summer
On the Fourth of July

Saving Mr. C

The day the signs in New York came down I realized
I had to save the Cookie Monster
From the sad lot of putrid purple people
Who idiotically, politically correctly
Call themselves adults.
Forgetting the joy in life that can be found in a cookie.
That simple pleasure,
Children for decades have been chasing, reaching,
Raiding, pillaging, and plundering
The kitchen cabinets for, late at night.
That thing, shared in the kitchen between brothers and sisters
In the slow, succulent victory
Over adults who think there is so much that is unhealthy.
They forget, living with no joy for the sake of health is worth nothing.
Especially not the destruction of a small, introverted creature
Whose job includes introducing the letter C, the world-over
Trying to control himself while chewing up sets, in search of his one joy.
After all, we do not shoot the Grouch for being grouchy,
Or commit Big Bird for talking to
Big brown Snuffleupagus who hides himself from the eyes of others.
So, why take it away from The Cookie Monster?
Cookie Madness is part of us, even in the dark.
Losing that is like losing those slow perfect moments when we are alone
And realize we can walk again amongst the stars
That color-us-in like a box of crayons.
And removing them simply because we forgot how to make sense
of the night sky.

It seems so self-destructive to our nature.
To take that from the future makes me wonder what is next.
I place my three-year-old son,
(Who thinks he's gotten the upper-hand in outsmarting me concerning that
extra snack), Crumbs on his Rocket Racer pajamas,
Into bed,
Beside the blue fur of a companion that keeps him from harm,
From the nightmares the world brings.

NPR

I wake for the morning to the sound
Of the elk herd trampling the side of my house
And the kitchen radio old and silver with it's one speaker sputters
"You're listening to National Public Radio"

Sounds of my mother in the shower dangle in the
Background
One of three eventual pairs of socks is placed on the kitchen island
I hear the words "All Things Considered" play out before breakfast
Or before the sun rises
And a man by the name Robert Siegal says
"We now send you over to Washington
To have a deeply philosophical discussion about what is going on in
Our nation's capital"

Meanwhile mother has come out of the shower with dad behind her
Where apparently she too
Has been listening, and the nine-year-old me, wants to ask her
What does this broadcast all mean? and what does Bob Edwards look like?
Why does Terry Gross know so much?
Do all families have this morning ritual or is it just ours that is listening?

A segment reveals Nelson Mandela has just been elected president
Of some far-off place in South Africa after being released from prison
And just knowing his name
Makes me feel I am alive,
Bearing witness to the impossible
My brain thanks this team of people who understand
The power of unbiased perspective.

The stories continue even though Diane Rehm's retires
and Nina Totenberg loses her friend, the supreme court judge
Yet the ritual of engagement is not lost
Even now communing with raccoons on my deck

Just a Thought on My Hero Charlie Brown

I wonder most
In the dark sleep of life
About the story of a small boy
Standing in spite of all the indignity of the
World
While holding his head up
As best he can, against all
The self-doubt brought by others,
Who have named him a
Blockhead
Searching for simple, delicate things
Grass and dandelions in spring,
A baseball game that turns
To the season,
Of
The simple struggle
To find the courage
To talk to a little red-haired girl
When all the others say
 Forget it kid!

An 80's Kid Cruises Colfax

The birthing sky breaks
The Ramones introduce me to the kids
With blue and green hair
Shaping my world like a bright red mohawk
As "Bonzo Goes to Bitburg,"
And I (who share the nickname Bonzo) fight "The Man"
Splattering art and anarchy
To create a breath of love
In an acid identity, washed and spun in my birth
Somewhere between California and the Old West
Where the summer sun beats down on me in a Clash
The fast-paced version of "I fought the Law and the Law Won"
Plays telling me "this will catch up with you"

But in this moment, I am free;
Free from mom, free from dad
To watch some movie called
"Over the Edge"
And kiss a girl deeply with my hands on her butt in the basement
Because I am alive
And I can, even though her dad will try to kill me over it later.

Oh, to be punk, once
Oh, to be "Sedated" at CBGB's
Oh, to be an artist trying to figure it out poetically
The kids in my tribe coming and going
On their way to letting it all go

I think I am grateful I got any action back then.

Cruising Colfax on the way to a late-night cup of black coffee
At a Diner of Destiny

Grandpa's Library

The books stare at me in their wonder
An alien cat man in a space helmet, or Dinosaur Beach
A pathway to the strange unknown
Where I learn of the scientific fictional dreamers
Who take me to strange new worlds
Pages of Anne McCaffrey's Dragon Books
Ray Bradbury, or Phillip K Dick
Shaping me in my

Wonder of ancient galaxies, and the stories
Of time travel making a space boy
Of beauty

A traveler in the night
I make but a spot on the floor,
Curled up with a blanket
To find your family's copy of
Alexei Panshin's *Rite of Passage,*
To learn the names Isaac Asimov, Robert Heinline,
Or the thousands of unknown
Who try to be sci-fi royalty

And yet I learn life's lessons
In this way, making me want to know more
About the people of the red planet
And where my place is on
This great voyage that takes us
Toward the stars

But now it is bedtime, for the grandson
Who longs for another page.

Cow Jumped Over the Moon By: Sean Keating

A Self Portrait
(For My Brother Sean)

The boy in blue skin
Wearing polka-dotted boxer shorts
Floats through space heroically
Trying to save my day in his self-portrait.

Riding a tutu-wearing hypo
He controls with a fishing pole,
His demented cow jumps over the moon,
Fascinating his little brother,

Helping create an identity of heartfelt sarcasm
In the artistic unknown.
Albums our parents never told us about play.
They create a music language,
For our journey of time together
And we hold on to what's left of home.

The world changes from mountains to apartment complexes,
We cruise in a silver spaceship car.
My sibling makes me a mixed tape of punk for my first girlfriend,
Driving, asking the question, "where are two comic book geeks to find
Home?"
Amongst the insanity of divorce
Posing the question, "what dimensions are we to go traveling in?"

In my stillness I remember our journey, word-for-word

That made our warped sensibilities.

Fallingwater:
(For the Architect)

Tracing paper is shaping
Perfection in the evening sunset
Against the rocks, and dripped in
The perception of natural existence amongst the falls.
The old man, through his glasses, with his charcoal covered hands,
Sketched you endlessly, shaping the family home
As students collapse in the unique style of
Art personality brought to life.
The people come and go,
Houses are designed,
And the joints ache a bit, but still are a wheel of curiosity, of image.

Things to Consider in Breaking Wind:

Tasting terribly blue breaths,
Sounds softly dancing dangerously,
Casting for catfish, in unwanted ways,
Hinting on heated suggestion.

A jolly old joke, Grandma and Grandpa's lift—
Symbolic and sensitive,
Often soft in the cataclysmic creation,
A special snore, thank god for the open door.

On Rover's nose two flies lift
In search of some place
Tattered, worn yet still,
Closer to the breeze,

And my wife with a cold
Turn of the deadly shoulder
Says thank you for giving up
The bean-dip and beer.

Just a Moment: An Ode on the American Twentieth Century
(To David Mamet)

And so it was, he screamed "Big Fat Hippo Dick",
Overwhelmed
In the bicycle repairman's journey at Kitty Hawk,
When the lights went out
In the ball fields of old Chicago and New York,
The end of Americans caring about batting practice,
Businesses rattled out pension plans to fathers who had come of age,
You could hear the breath, the days, and the moments
That had lived. Wrapped in plain brown paper
Engraved pocket watches passed down to kids
Metaphors similes, and history books,
It was moments crafting art out of soup cans,
And memorials sadly made from piled shoes, and black granite
Chiseled names,
With crowning achievements of Gen-Xer's
Who like their magic boxes never knew the world without
The quick touch of the Golden Arches,
Yes, it was confirming our addictions, to
Diet, caffeine free, and clear, black liquids poured from
A can of cola, and Alka-Seltzer
Yes Sir! I praise it all, from jingles, to the problems of our pet rock,
To red Noids
Who sold us slices, prices, and maximum relief?

But to know freedom we watched a hockey team,
The miracle, of how all of America was a dream
To question
"Were we all children walking on the moon,
That was once made out of cheese?"

Part II. Life

Self-Portrait by: Sean Keating

A Thought on Berkley Breathed

I had a conversation with Milo Bloom,
Talking the talk, walking the walk,
Un-cooly of course,
"Coke or Pepsi?"
But more importantly, we talked
About the importance of the little things,
Such as the laughter we all forgot,
Our hearts missing
The high and mighty Basselope.
Gambling on go-fish,
We bantered politically
Incorrect about our favorite dish.
Nine years old going on thirty
Milo and me.
We talk about how women
Ain't not sex objects,
But they sure is pretty.
So we pass our notes
And I ask him why he asked
That woman if she ate her baby.

The Engineer

Staring into the
Dark whisper of the tired night,
The nature of his hand rests
On the troubled cup of coffee,
Encased in resentful Styrofoam,
He ticks and it bubbles containing
The black substance that holds
So much power over him.
The mechanical, The electrical,
Ticking to achieve a harmonic purity:
The light of his human nature disappearing
To reveal the child he is, sitting alone
Counting the starlight.

Notice the Coyotes

In the fields of Indian-Paintbrush,
Colored in the woven yarn of red sweaters
Worn by children hiding amongst the yellow stalks of grass,
The howls of the southwest grow.
They are covered in the dense invisibility of the plateau.
Across the road, the kindness
Given to the dog by comparison
Is made apparent by
Water in his silver metal bowl
And the rifle leaned against the porch.
The smell of the chicken coop makes
The air seems blood filled.
The white steeple of an abandoned church washed
And chipped in the dust tells sinners
The frontier is at an end.
The tame wild will not be
                         Wild.
"Glory halleluiah"
To the pack of muscles unleashing
Themselves into a power of movement
Like a crack and thunder in the trickery
Of Pueblo basket weavers who
Dye images of the shape under a moon,
Selling them at the farmers market,
Amongst clay pottery.
A pelt, skinned and hung,
Drapes next to the coon-skin hats

For tourists.

Rage the departed hunter feels
In snatching the air that bursts into the body,
To bring the numbered dead justice
In the white footed pursuit of pray,
Whose demise lingers as the taste of tequila in a preacher's mouth
While a member of a local flock is digested into scat
That protects in its fragrant smell

The birth of a windbreak
Otherwise girdled
By the sharp vagrant descendants of a rat.

By: Conor Keating

Warped

And one day the Christian Woman asked me what I believed
As a man in this day and age,
And this is what I told her, my take on Culture:
That I was completely down with communing with the Big J.C
But that in terms of moral compass I was inclined, in this modern age
Of grace, to listen to the horrified beautiful truth
From communing with The Spirit, in the theater alone
Where space-ships shoot and destroy the universe
Amongst creatures colored green
And men dressed in black, who wave red and green swords,
That we worshiped in our youth while waving flashlights in mimicry.
These images define morality with more relevancy
Than a big book containing a burning bush drawn in boredom.
She can read her Bible and whisper it all but at the end of my day,
My morality is defined in realizing
My skate-shoes are used for skating and not being cool
And the Pacific San Diego Ocean is how I commune
With the creator, standing out across the water,
No civilization in sight as the green flash stares back at me.
The mall has just as much excitement as the church place.
People go back and forth, back and forth forgetting
It's not my job to satisfy them but me in designing my styled existence.
And thoughts about my generation?

Optimus-Prime voices play inside my head
While I think about
Buying my cousin Cobra Commander so, he, too can
Understand that terrorists are absurd people in costumes
Who Scheme, thinking they are hurting everyone,
But really, we're insane to be afraid of the things we can't control.
Lost in this experimental concentration, I now wander.

Comic-book stores are where I think,
And as I think communing with the coffee-drip liquid of Stan Lee
I hear the power of my mythos. Stan can't you just
Understand they just don't understand me?
I relate to the world through the adventures of
Spaceman Spiff, The Avengers, and Shakespeare characters

Cast out on an island. It is this that I am to be,
But they just don't get it I think,
Because I just don't believe.

A Writer's Storm

A writer writes in a wild thunderstorm
Of imagination
Shifting like a desert rattle snake
As he tries to break free
Loving deeply and passionately
A moment from the Old West
A flash of Billy the Kid riding
Into the soul like lightning in Santa Fe
Where the cactus blooms in a moment of moisture
Against one's skin
On a Navajo reservation

Live young,
Die young
In the saddle
He writes, his way to freedom,
Sipping a glass of whiskey in the stops along the way
The word "Pals" etched in the journal for all of history
The existential enemies shoot bullets, upon boxes of bullets into
The air, trying to stop him from completing his ride on the trail

Ride into the storm,
Ride with the moment of the tumble-weed,
Ride one last moment with the Regulators
Who are not forgotten

Even now, that they are nothing more than the rise of a grain of dust
Amongst the smell of cattle and the canyons of New Mexico

Write cowboy, write your legend
In the washing of your soul
To find home in the creek waters
And peace where the poem meets the
Page as he looks out into the sunset

Inventions of the Down and Dirty Kid who Calls Himself:
A Skate-boarder

Concrete Beauty spinning in fading light of the sun once more,
The hills, breaking, perfect formats of riding on the waves,
With precision movement in life, opening a gliding door,

In hypnosis of a day kids will soar,
It's all the style behind a man and the attention he craves
With precision movement in California, opening a gliding door

Surfing aesthetically the asphalt shore,
Graphic culture hidden in dying caves
With precision movement in art, opening a gliding door

Zephyr kids hanging to become philosophical folklore,
Pure freedom before the corporate slaves,
Concrete beauty spinning in fading light of the sun once more

     Dog-Town style to the core
     Leaving Jay Adams to tend my many graves,
     As beauty, in concrete surf, spinning in light of the sun once more,

     The radical nature of jungle-land-city roar,
     In harvesting the wasteland we will ever ride the waves,
     Concrete beauty spinning in fading light of the sun once more,
     Waking precision movement, artists, opening a gliding door.

By: Sean Keating

Photo of John Alley Wall by: Robin Sarf and Lisa Sarf

Welcome to Moscow! Idaho

Driving in from the north and the west the signs read,
"Welcome to Moscow Heart of the Arts"
 I'm in my 20's
Where driving downtown the words ask
What versions of existence do we see when we say
Welcome to America?
Welcome to Moscow!
The place where people who interpret in the manner
Of a French salon, coming together implanting, entrapping
The non-cooking part of a panhandle, contemplating, a future
That doesn't suck. While the indebted, launch forward
To avoid a life in the nitty-gritty trailer-park
On the north side of town that crashes and burns down
Like unemployed Winger's cooks basking in the booze.

Welcome to Moscow!
Where we've got the unemployed, the near employed,
The employed until next season, the fighting-for -a -future
Here and there sort of employed,
Jazz musicians, and coffee shops galore,
Styled and tiled, brewed up and chewed up, defending that extra mile
A difference in downtown style,
Christian mission, family owned and hip,
Each serving a different pastry with Cool-Whip.

Welcome to Moscow!

Home of the original sensation creational Robot Dance party,
Put on by bagel boys, and people posing to be bartenders.
They move and groove in the summer time riding bikes
Down to the slow Tuesday of insanity at the local Ale House
Passing bars, where we've got bills,
And Bills, from Alaska who used to swim but now enjoy, choir songs,
Johns who mingle in the pool hall, and saxophone Mikes
Who keep their daughters safe,
With a Corner Club where you can throw peanuts on the floor.
Topped off with Plant' specials, a fishbowl and
Percolating Sound of Slurp and Burp during a Bovill Run,

Ping pong Bars with popcorn, and deep-fried cheese
Welcome to the scene!
Where we've got architects, lawyers, freaks, geeks, artists, wannabe's,
Hippies, of all kinds, educated people there for the Sixties,
And those who are just too damned stoned to find their feet.

Some of them juggle fire
Sitting outside playing drums
Celebrating the good times.
Yes, the characters are all posing as people.

We've got Mollys,
Sarahs, Carmens, Courtneys, Tonys, Witneys and Tabithas,
Old-school and new-school Christian's, Jew's,
And people who practice the Koran, all in sin, who yell
At those sitting in peace petting Buddha on the belly.

The Scow

It's wild, child, and a little Mexico too for those sailing in from the
Palouse.
We've got cheap beer, mixed with expensive taste,
But damn straight, the quality here for the most part is first rate.
Where I am Parking it in-front of a professor, who writes and writes and
Writes,
And those books she writes are hip cool books,
That talk about the sexy seductive side,
The black skirt and high heel side of life.
After all, we are a down-on-jazz town, and jazz means "the sex."
Hanging in the Social Club, way up above,
Just up the street
From Mama's Joint martini and an elegant Red-Door.

Welcome to Moscow!
Where we've got
Cocaine, broke down shame, and dark sides,

Total painted artists, skate kids, and damn huckleberry pickers,
Who torture their five-year-old kids in the process.
Of being alive. Babies bathe naked

In the downtown fountain.
When it's hot
We find,
Toms and Aftons to tell us about the war, and what it's not,
Veterans and other tales too are here in the Scow as
People are thinking about bending, smashing, and arguing
With good hearts,
America with their politics, and not so politic agendas,
You think "Welcome to Moscow!"
Where wheels spin in this moderately damaged brain,
Nectar sipped, in mouths of grownup frat-boys, who remember rides
In golden bowls yelling yo-ho,
Wandering from blue-houses to our brown-house under the moon.
The stories are of light and fights broken out,
Stories known as legends to the small children of 18 who listen.
Articles of Playboy Magazine, professionals at what you say?
Welcome to Moscow we shout in whisper,
Just another day of boredom, I guess,
The weather has turned kind of cloudy and gray
Thinking of *Ulysses*. With sushi delicacies,
I say welcome to Moscow where hell breaks loose
In more ways than one,

Shadows and Billboards light the street,

Broadcasting
Radio Free, Kenworthy
And county fairs.

As we continue on in search of a taste…
Watch out for the Plinker bomb.

Welcome to Moscow!

Where if you haven't seen it
Get out and shout!
Bilingual, single, tinkle in the ocean, sound of vibration
Tough, rough, and original
Combating what's to come,
Shaking up everything

With melting pot thought.
And now I'm on my way,
I'm on my way.
Cowboy hat falling apart,
As I head off into the grass
Single, dignified, with chai on the side.
Welcome to this part of America.

Downtown Moscow by Robin Sarf and Lisa Sarf

The Swing Dance

I remember it vividly the day I used up the last of my courage
  To learn to Dance…
I pressed each foot left and right with a rock step
And a weight shift as I stood alone in the school gym, awkward
 and scared, trying to learn what it was like to live again.
After all, I was just trying to get back on the railroad tracks.
  After the storms of life
  That we all experience tore me up
  And spat me out into a spittoon on the Chew Tobacco Rag!
Leaving me like John Steinbeck's visionary turtle
Pushing down the highway in the dust, feeling like
A down-on-his luck average Joe, stuck on America's ride

But…
It was only so simple, I simply had to stay calm in the movement,
Going alone as time and dreams shook
The radio-waves of my awkward American youth boy culture,
 To call up the start of this
Shadowed moon-lit sound
                    hiding in the dark corners of the club …
The Sachmo sound!   I heard
Crawling down the spine like a spider
The trumpet whose breath of air cast the way to freedom
 To hear it slowly drip into my mouth and ear
It began as Louis Armstrong touched me on the shoulder and said
This was going to be ok, if I had it in me to take this chance kid
And feel the rhythm and blues of his old-school

Mountain of cool cats, who played to the sound of the
Big Band small time Rhythm first hand
And there he was, Django Rinehart on the guitar, tapping it out
In gypsy dreams

And the flappers in white shoes beginning to flap
Tipping and tapping, tipping and tapping, and tipping
As the Charleston is profoundly pushed out into the shoes
Off the eight-count step

Amongst a circle of circled up dresses that are being so un-lady like,
A circle of dismay as interesting to watch as a Big B
With a Shorty George leap!

The lights, when I begin to get the steps right, flicker the
Eight-count, touch, stop, and ceremonies of the lamps to be lit in
Harlem as big street signs read the Savoy,
Competition sound where black and white come together to jam
Free from life's everyday dismay

Don't hold
The white suit Lindy-Hoppers breaking down the barriers of
What it feels like to Fly
Letting it all go away
  The voice of Ella Fitzgerald burning distinctive
  And unique as if the blood could just melt away.
The count starting on a one two rhythm, as you try to hold
The music inside
  To connect it all together with the feet.

Count Basie yelling out a one two three, as Chick Web yells
Back to the brass section as he stretches out
With his right hand, baton waving back
And forth back and forth, the click and clack of white shoes.
One band crashing down the stomp! the other taking it down slow.
Circle up, circle up and around I go

A Texas Tommy
Catching the incredible partner by the wrist… triple step and do it again
Then push forward as you begin to Shag the collegiate way
Like they used to do back in 1936, those crazy Harvard-Yale filled days
When Benny Goodman style was king
                                        Slow slow, fast
Fast steps,
Lifts in between,
With the signal being
A touch on the back,

The piano breaking it all down and the imagination

As the floor clears itself away
And the sound of gold-plated instruments shatters
                                    down the storm of the fast
Beat of Balboa
                        Those fascinating legs bend in seductive creation
A pause and go stop on every third step...of the movement
 Front to back pushing... and pulling yourself this way and that... way
The temptation of the devil inside turning the heat
Down the slow arch curve

Of a girl in a black dress, who presses her body against
Sound.
Crash and burn awkward kid, crash and burn,
'Cause she now is looking you in the eye and wants to dance,
Turning you over and looking you up and down
"Do you have a partner, because you do now" they say.

Count it out count it out count it out, count it out,
Don't go too fast don't go too fast, breathe, breathe,
Take it in, just a slow step
Realize there is absolutely no need to apologize
As you feel her breath, turn with perfection,
Take all that courage I've, you, me, got left
                                    And dip
 Making sure to catch it all.
Catch it all
Just catch it all kid, and take it in.

In response to Elizabeth Bishop's "The Moose"

In dark, decay on the siding
From the houses of the city
Of a small town, a bus travels west
As it were the nature of such things,
 A disappearance from lake houses
Lit in kind by what appear as paper lanterns on porches
Off into the pastures of red farmhouses
Followed by
A summer memory flashing
In the image of a loon landing on the water
A return to etiquette and proper punctuation
A fall term at University
A Student in a tweed blazer, boarding with a duffle bag
And penny loafers shined with a rag
A wheel in movement conducts the setting, to wooded
Leafy green lushness of a forest
In motion at the setting of a day's
Turn from mid-afternoon to evening
Distractions where an old couple in right old fashion
Clammer aboard with a secretary of sorts at the next stop,
A guitarist, a soldier in uniform, quiet and confident solemness,
A mother lost in a purse, a father wondering when he will find a job
All looking at and greeting each other

One hears the voices of
Passengers that ask
"What if he dies in the war?"
"How is he managing
Now that the factory has closed?"
"Has her son failed out and taken to fishing out in the ocean?"
"Her blue haired child was just misunderstood"
He took to drink
She had left him indefinitely
She had transferred as a muse to New Orleans
The year the storm broke the levies

A dark, scratching air
Trees, both terrifying

And menacing, surround the outside slopes.
A gasp of a coyote in the distance
In the hollow wood
And time passes

Listening to the voice of the poet
He had not yet discovered on a literary passage given by a professor,
A divine rite of passage
In the bright light under the stars

Reading the words
Over, and over again
"A moose has come out of the impenetrable wood

And his eyes loom there
Other-worldly,
Crying, as he tries to hold back tears,
It's alright now,

A departure from a cocoon of a man
To the library
As a breath of cold air touches his other senses he departs.
Because a moose lingers in a memory
The way all of us find simplicity.

Part III. WAR

Untitled by: Sean Keating

The Purple Chicken by : Solar Dunn

In the Bag
(For Orson Welles and Jeff MacNelly.)

Purple chicken heading out
For take-off on the street,
Neighbor nosy, do you have purple chickens
That bounce and flop to make your life complete?
Watch out for the purple chicken fleet
So unrefined, unskilled in aerial ballet.
With Hula-Hoops and grenades
They waddle on in whacked parade
Shouting and pouting in their deep-fried rampage.
Turn your radios up and be alert
One just ate this reporter's shirt.
Put down that bran muffin,
Repeat these are not cute and fuzzy birds
Such as the lovable irresistible puffin.

They are mad I tell you, mad
And viciously obese,
Kamikazes with crash-and-burn courses.
They attack terrible and random
Like a bad rhyme on horses,
Missiles on calculated trajectories
Like insurance salesmen sitting with a phone directory.
On the spot like that! They took out Col. Sanders,
Sending him to his plot.

The guard decided just in case this story was not a prank
To mobilize the troops, load the guns, and feather dust the tank.
Pin feathers, wing tips, and gully fluff
Fog-horn Leghorn joins the fray.
It's me and Shoe in the trenches
And the tide of this conundrum isn't turning our way.

To Washington the purple poultry proceed.
A crap-splattered cloud of
White gooey guano descending
Down Pennsylvania Avenue
To make their life a matter for the court.
"Rights For Chickens" filed in report.

Their existence revealed as a science project
Gone awry in 1822,
The birds run across the presidential lawn
The world as we know it has become a pawn!
I now see the creature in motion, they even inhabit the ocean!
"Good Night and Good Luck", recognizing the end
And watch as the sky is falling.

Library of a Flower Columbine
(2000)

I walked the grounds in the day
As a cold breath of wind blew in the distance.
The grim visage of a dark tower looking down from above,
The day full of books,
          Books which spoke our truths,
Our truths of our culture and our time,
What did the nation know of it?
After all, it was our flower to destroy,
Our tears to be,
Our intercoms to silence,
A year and to the day.
          Anger,
To walk where faces were no more,
Only in the books,
Only in their truth sealed
As I smoked the silence of the air,
A tomb as none I could imagine at 15
A list we, those kids of Jefferson County,
          Wish we had never read,
A card catalogue no longer so
Full and bitter at the names,
Etched in the pages,
The stories,
Even Eric's book was there
Resting.

Crosses Art Print   By: Paul Deardorff

A new century starts with another war:
(Return to "In Flanders Fields")

It is in these fine words,
Now I ask to be given back my breath,
In dignity walking a long time, alone I think
Forgiving each other for everything that has come and gone
In the divine trumpets of the children that look upon the
Forgotten fields of yesterday.
Lingering now with thoughts
Where the poppies once did blow
Between the crosses row on row,
We ask where does war go in the desert that
Chimes to the men below,
To the voices casting themselves
Forever upon the starlit-sunset sands
As brothers sing "Ring-Around- the-Rosie" to the
Children once united long ago
Underneath a single flag and moon
Of an Arabian empire.
The age of fear and terror lingering long since passed,
It seems to those at home,
Who see the snow of lost winters,
As a better day when we were with jobs and family
And could hold our heads without the anger of it all.

We whose voices who are now delicate
As the ticking of a wristwatch against the ear…
That must tick

To make it, ask simply this…

Can we make it right with the many books separating us from them?
Those who hide their faces, in clothes black and unharming to the skin,
Until we count the dead
Who now as boys and girls who once went outside
Wander to play baseball in the hour of the spring as
Earth the color of coffee
Is placed around their feet, happy it is over
Grounded slowly by recognition to the touch

Of some difference, in some different measure of morality
That balances what else might be left to say,
In the deserts of the east where we go
With one another
Row on row
Whispering, and as we whisper
Help us touch what we have learned,
This morning, this day
Where we look to love again,
In the sensation of the glowing dawn
That comes to shake the sadness
From restless hate in the days to come
Where we can live again
Free upon our shores to laugh as children do
Children at play once more
In games that can make us breathe
In the words like our Eternal Flame lit, and others
Who ask now for hope.

Vandal Shield by Robin Sarf and Lisa Sarf

A Mail Man's Morning

I.

I cannot see everything
In truth or but
What can a man in this day and age do to fight
To be himself, as he goes without family
Off to the predicament of breathing for a pay-check?
He is just a confusion of himself
Lost in the struggle of seeing
The world with hope
Gliding upon earth with
Imagination resting in the dirt.
Battling hell to find his place upon this
Shadow lit scull of life that is his to row,
Breaking every breath of expectation
Shattering every moment
With words that send him
Further and further from those
Who try to understand,
The cold breath of
Demons blue and wild
That haunt his dragons' wings,
That haunt the cracks of the inner inspiration,
But most often it is just this simple picture
That describes the struggle.

II.

A boy lost in the early hours of the morning
Wraps himself softly in a blanket,
The color of the rainbow pattern
Etched in red and green.
He climbs stairs with no sound uttered into the air
From the lungs that are pounding in his chest
To search for the creature in the shadows he knows as his father
The slow soft light of dignity coming from the kitchen
Grumbling about walking into the cold without his family
In the night before the sun rises
Which reminds him of what it feels to be human
For it will be many days before the figure

In the kitchen will glimpse daylight
In its full burning recognition that
It is as warm and nourishing to the soul
As the black cups of coffee that make
The drive possible to the prison,
And as the light fades out in the kitchen the boy is
Left wondering what he has just observed, but he is too late
To ask

Red Neck Fourth of July in Jersey

Three days left until the end according to the homeless man's
Cardboard sign
And the fire of God has yet to show up on my doorstep,
But CCR is playing on the radio,
And as I wonder what it is I'm celebrating on the Fourth of July
The fan turns itself over and over again in my direction
Seagull's poop on my hat that says "Darn Seagulss."
And the cooler is empty.

IRAQI Headline

Once more a good man rises in the storm
In hopes that the story in this sea
May take him across the bridge of dreamers
To count bottle caps and play stickball in the camp
While thinking of capital crimes, and how he might
Meet his end in a commemorable way
Equal to any hero crossing upon the ancient shores of Troy,
In the desert of desperation,
Yet perhaps there is hope
For his killing nature as
We read the last printed headline on yesterday's thrown out newspaper,
Telling the tale of an Army boy,
Homesick and smelling of gasoline
Who looks a child in the eyes
As he hands over a chocolate bar and says
"Forgive me."

2025

The wood is on fire,
As I look deep into your eyes of blue and recall
"Our Better Angels" and wonder where she is,
As I remember to be human
To be kind and to be a creature of love.
To be a man holding on to love,
And loving so deeply that there is a place where hate cannot go
As the Nazi paint infects the skin.
The skin of those who fear the others
Who fear me because I will not be silent
To the way they treat her.
It hurts inside to think she who is my wood and my world
Is left broken and torn sitting in the field struggling to find a voice
That will bring hope to the hopeless divide

And the wood is on fire,
But her people are not dead
Even if she's changing in the dark,
And her moon is eclipsed by the voices of the hunters.
Yet, if I wait for just a moment in this moment
I can see in her the good that cannot be taken
As the darkness also must pass

For Stephen Colbert

       It was a revival of survival the way the Americans
Stopped World War III.
Like all good things it started in Hollywood
In a meeting involving a draft of "Caddy-shack Three"
You know, the one where the caddies win again,
While a room of writers stoned and alone decide to
Take the advice of late-night talk show hosts galore
To interpret the words "Make America Great Again"
To mean an American dream with a cultural scene
Where the people chant with success while looking into
The sun shouting bring back the gays and while we are at it
Let's bring back Mel Brooks to Broadway
And the Kennedy Center
With so much winning, that there was and is, no delay
And beyond
As we the people watch the country sing, jive, and escape from
From others in pointy white hats,
Delighting in celebration remembering how
Robin Williams and Billy Crystal
Seized our day
With Whoopi – never forget Whoopi –
In dance fever and beyond as our people's hips
Gyrated like Elvis
With one for the money two for the show and three honey let's go with
No more merchandise!

For the love of our dance partners, with consent
Canada and Mexico we asked for a halt
On a thousand percent tariff
On forgiveness and Pancakes.
We the people find it absurd to put a tariff on compassion
Without making sure
Breakfast at the meeting of our people, coming together. Working as one
Is complimentary for all
Since we the people know cooking eggs is
Of the people,
 And by the people
 And of great concern for the people

So say the backstage writers and fighters
Who with a hug and a kiss
Thicken the plot in Act II
And get together with the nations
Of Care Bears
Especially Ukrainian Share Bear
And Russian No Heart Bear
Figuring out for the people down below
That if we all care a lot about each-other, we win
Especially a gold star,
But that's how our American people did it
Returned to the land of "The New Deal."

Watonga Oklahoma

I watch the giant snapping turtle walk the road of desperation
Kissing you as deeply as I can under the Oklahoma sun
In a moment where and oilman shoots me in the back because
I'm disposable
And the dog in his yard saves my life
Telling me to take home his hungry mud-stained hide of black
To play with the chickens and the armadillos
That make me wonder where Tony Hoagland,
Writer of excellent wit is now,
It was his words that made me daydream
When the guns of an Iraqi desert killed my generations' innocence
And now all I want to do is cook you dinner
In a thunderstorm that smells of change

Part IV. Love

Japanese Print By: Paul Deardorff

The Trout Man
(for Robert Wrigley)

And so it was the trout-man
Shaped in the depths of nature
Who told me
The way to a woman's heart
You truly love
Is to write her

Write her poems he said in his still voice
That was aged in wisdom like a bottle of backwoods whisky
Distilled and poured delicately into a cup of ice
Teaching me poetry
In my youth
The images of Richard Hugo's Montana
The mystery of the mountain landscape that one captures in a breath
And birds flocking to him to be shaped in a creative quatrain

Specifically, I remember the eloquence of his
Anthropomorphic Duck that flew into the air
Or the brief passage from "The Moon in the Mason Jar"
From an early work

But mostly
As if he truly understood me,
I remember he asked who had captured my heart
As a young man

In that northern landscape of writers
The way the trout hangs in the water
Swallowing the line
Pulling and dragging
Hoping to be reeled in
With a breath, at the surface

For it was his rhythm that calmed me so,
As
I jumped into the channel
Of the smooth clear trickle

Watching the line
With a fly on the end
I told him, confessing my secret
And he looked at me
With a smile and said
"Ah, yes
I remember her well."

The pen continues on
In that bright lit moment
In my journal where fish spawn
In a delicate swish upon a river
And her hair, red as though it were a stripe
Rests gently upon a shoulder far away

In her study
Where she now sits
Ever a wonder to me
Amidst the smell of coffee that surrounds
The taste of bacon from a campfire
Against the silhouette
Of early morning
Before I, ever a student,
Touch the creative waters and cast away

Foil Art Photography By: Paul Deardorff

To Pause

  I read the works of Yeats
On this thunder-mug,
This fifteen-minute crapper,
I paid a quarter to use.
In an answer to my prayers,
In the bus station, with a found moment
For contemplating
The Lord's existence
In the art of relieving myself.

While in the stall next to me
An Orthodox rabbi from Pensacola
Talks about golf statistics
With words tingling off the tip

Of the tongue, to form an ode on stanzas,
The puddle of words a mirror of droplets
That form a distinct impression,
As I am collapsing, on my Nikes.

The graffiti tells stories
Of the places I have been
The hearts that read
For a good time call
Mary Ann scribbled in pen.

Yet as I stare at a chain
Around the holiest of holy scrolls
That gives so much comfort
No tongue but some cheek—
The faint sounds of a father

Giving a blessing for
Goldie the goldfish, who died,
A carnival prize,
A take home special,
Echoes in the screams
Of little Fredrick
I hear through the wall.

And all this time I am
Contemplating the cap and bells,
But in this, like the stories of
Mark Twain, I fear the overflow
And I leave the painted
Blue box that hides me away in safety.

Stoner

Chilly Willy cartoons,
Chinese, marijuana,
And chopsticks
Tickling the surface
Of my cave of laundry
Bogged down by the weight
Of Wisconsin Mac and Cheese
Bubbling in my bachelorhood
 I'm too tired to be understood
 But interrupted by the phone's ring.

Fire

The fire of water,
The fire of man,
The fire of Brotherhood!
The fire of the Sun!
The fire of the Dead!
The fire of being alone,
The fire of the heart.
The fire of the calculations.

How cliché is fire
When there is talk of flesh?
And how cliché is water
When there is the talk of life?

And why does a record
Needle placed
In the hands of a child
Still touch in precise seduction,
The skin of an old broken
Section of vinyl,

The dust lifted into the air
By the cataclysmic sound
Of a band who made
The boy's mother remember
How gently the mud dripped down
Her skirt in 1968 as she held
Her husband's hand firmly
Against her breast.

Fall

Words worn as my old suede jacket
Often look in the morning a comfort
To the traveler in the wind,
To remember the water,
Which drips slowly upon my hand,
Just as I looked upon her face, in autumn
The slow touch of art a simple jazz balloon
Floating in the complicated afternoon.
Then watching her from
Across the street the wind touches my lips
Taking the burning of the first moment's cigarette away.
I ask sometimes,
But this is a story of an evening where I wandered
To find the rhythm of our breath
Simple, for love can mean only so much
On the road.
Yet, there I am,
Afraid
Maybe this was

Collage of Palouse by: Robin Sarf and Lisa Sarf

Search for the Wild

The sunset looked at us
The truck drove into the dark
Winding existence,
Was in rhythm with the thought of
The earth at peace with itself.
Making sense of a brush-stroked sky,
I watched the woman next to me.
Her hair floating in the gap between the window and the wild.
It lifted gently in the wind
And I felt the wild was a place we feared,
Yet I still marveled at it.

Our Dodge breathed in the smell of oil
Mixed in thickness of what little air there was

Throughout the old cab from our hand me down
The mosquitoes, moving on the road, seeming to slow as they sparkled
In their death.
The fields of rolling hills engulfed our tiny truck,
And pulled us away from the white picket image
Of a home in the suburbs that people like us looked to for comfort,
While the guitar of an old folk song played on the radio
Amongst our mundane natures.
Breaking that quiet crisp moment,
The flick of a cigarette escaped,
Making a torch of blue fire
That touched the fields.
Her and I let go of controlling the journey

In the backcountry of the rolling Palouse.
With the growing color
Our eyes focused on the wheat turning
To ethereal images of light,
Which to this day recalls
Youthful time spent with someone of significance,
A kind of rift that serves to remove my life of predictability.
My hand wrapped around hers
As we watched the change
Of the wheat change to dark ash

Feeling like adulthood crashing
Into our inabilities, revealing the truth

We felt nothing was expected of us.
It was fire, it was life, and yet so much more
In the confusion that was
A farmland birth.

Vandal Photo of Face and Shield by: Robin Sarf and Lisa Sarf

Pakistan in Idaho

I am found in an iridescent
Wonder of imagination
Blooming forth in this
American Madness of the West,
Abused and rebirthing residue
In the Lazarus Pit.
Eloquent frustration retrieved from
The furnace of joyous explosion.
I am holding you, the people,
Looking,
Dripping, dreaming, begging
To the starlit Redneck Savior
That so many people call God.
My life turning
Into the river
Whose depths wake the senses.
And in quiet,
I hear the breath of Pakistan catching
Fire in the pale, blue moonlit
Moments amongst the groves of dates
That occupy young men's minds,
Dangling in the crisp calculating cataclysm
Of youthful incense as fields of poppies bloom.
The words, perhaps,
Touch our sensations

Like the woman in a black veil who
Levels the imagination with her
Eyes in sensual curiosity

Who we can imagine as a child
In homemade robes,
Dancing in the waters of the
Caspian.
Words becoming a delight,
Seeing the smells of jasmine
And Turkish teas
That are boiled in the garden

Frog Talk

Dear Kermit the Frog,

      I hope your words will guide a fool such as me.
After all, it was you who said "it's not easy being green."
As I sit alone in a bus station at the crossroads
A tattered knap-sack full of dreams,
I wonder if I should just hit the open road of life,
Leaving my home behind
With my favorite bear in the front seat telling terrible jokes
While giving his brother's Studebaker to the Electric Mayhem.
Yes I could take this thought that a boy takes in his youth
And just how foolish would I have to be
To listen to the words of others in my thoughts and feelings
That I would leave that knap-sack
To fall to the earth
To be lost forever.

A Piano

Dust of a creature's mouth
Catches as a breath
Of air enters slowly.
Body opens, revealing
Bones that in truth reveal
Scales—
Scales who harmonically
Shape our life.

Hammers of its belly
Thunder and crack
Pattern woven together,
Black and white, pulling and pushing to
Create the sounds of color that drip
Wonderfully, like paint into
Our ears.

Then…
Stepping on toes
Sounds…
Linger
One more moment before the sleep,
So even the blind
Are left with something to see.

My Simonetta Cattaneo

I am old now but I remember how I looked on you
A youth in love with the lady of the joust
And the passionate dreams of the Botticelli paint that dripped.
Dances of Italian inspiration catching the divine
When da Vinci dangled in your imagination
Before the crossing moon set on a poet of Florence
That in stillness would listen to the poems
You wrote often and in good rhythm recall the moment .

Now, I find my way back to you.

Biology

Dear dead fertile black male cat
I met embalmed on the biology table,
You were closer to me than many of my friends during high-school.
We stared into each other's eyes fulfilling a promise of
Achieving a letter of satisfaction
That the teacher would not give.
I accidentaly, while looking at your teeth at six am,
Was responsible for breaking your jaw
With a set of clamps made of steel.
Maybe I spent too much time in the classroom staring at you,
Examining anatomy, scientific inquiries, studying your eyes,
Angering that person I took to prom by not showing up on time
Because of you.
But then again, maybe it's better this way,
No more awkwardly painful nights of bad sex for the women in our lives.

To Her I Love:

Little red sweatshirt girl
I fell in love with at the bus-stop of life
Where are you going in such a hurry?
Blond hair, toughness,
And a tennis racquet to be cast aside,
I'm sorry if I'm in your way but a boy
Dyslexics call The Dog put me here accidently
I think all nervous and twitching as I am
Inhaler in hand, to say
I don't suppose you see me like I see you?

Mountain Town

Living in an old mountain town
I hear the strings of Bonnie Raitt
"Angel from Montgomery" the soundtrack
Of the pool hall,
Writing you a poem
I will send with a stamp
Looking at your faded picture
Reading a penciled note, you gave me
Thinking how time has passed in
The life of this poet you inspired.
Hoping you never give up on me
Even if I'm lost like a horseman trying to find his way to water
Earning a pocket-full of change
Doing what
I can to try and tell you I love you

Part V. After

Fibonacci Spiral by Robin Sarf and Lisa Sarf

In Remembrance of the Punk Dennis Phelps

Hold your head with pride as you listen
To the sound of Hot-Water Music
Where a leader of deciphered dreams
Dives one last time into the pool
A pinup girl holds his studs
As he does the breast stroke
And hits it out of the park
Picking her up along the way
With a putter to match
He's a punk to trust
All truth and dignity as
His guitar displays the inner light
That has shined since the age of 12
He reminds us to
Never sell out
But instead drift to an authenticity
While embracing the issues of the day
To make us feel alive
With a wildness that is freeing
In the quest to live for passions
In life's moments
As those left behind to tap a keg, with a toast to a man gone too soon.

The Lonesome

In the heart of a West now gone
Where the grass burns in the yellow sun
An old cowboy looks once more
Out into the shadows among the tumble weeds
At all that was.

The sounds of buffalo
Slowly disappear
In the afternoon,
In search of the horsewoman
He left in Santa Fe,
He loved by a creek.

His hands are now aged like paper,
Torn with time,
The regret of a life lived alone dangled at his side like a gun.
Alone,
A ghost amongst the graveyard.

To Bucksnort

Smoke from the kitchen looms in the air creating a shadow,
A young boy sits on the porch playing a harmonica
His grandfather gave him.
Tourists seldom come to this town anymore.
A small strand of shacks off the road
At the base of cliffs, yet to a set of locals, who slide down
From their mountain hideaways for
Comfort and friendship, it is something more.
Fire and glow of the Bucksnort
Is a spirit like an old Indian woman whose hands weave clay in flames.
Fire that cooks the ski bum's supper on Saturday evening
Stirs in the corner and warms his feet,
Scent of hot buttered rum
Malt beer hangs in the air.
Wafting to the bear's nose
Whose soft body, resting as a rug, warms the bare feet of the children.
Children who, splashed ever so excitedly in the cool creek below
Playing games.
Water is a whisper
As it trickles and the trout hover in the pool
Aged cook's special soup has a taste.
As big as the grin on her wrinkled upper lip.
Her silent comment known to them all as a small wonder.

Joe Recalls His Last Day on Coney Island

The silken like quality in the beauty of the wrinkled hand holding a
Cigarette was all that I could imagine
Looking at the empty seat on the bench covered in our laughter,
Once fought over when
We were Kids
It was the place I thought I would sit forever
Watching the gulls chase bread in my memory
On Coney Island
That amazing place
One goes to find
Seniors who in the prime of life do underwater ballet in the morning
Before gently floating down the pier
To catch Cotton Candy on their tongue
One last time
But the voice is now calling me away
It's time to go I think
Into the water
To talk of card games and socializing
To tell her
I'm sorry but
I won a few more tickets
At Skee Ball
And I had to redeem them for time
With those I will come to miss
Watching the epic struggle of life

But I'll be there soon.

Watch

My father said what was left of my family was an old watch.
I had no Idea what he meant at the time.
It was perhaps the cold-hearted ticking
That seemed so perfect, which defined us
The gold-plated case smiling deceiving us in its lie.
Gold plating
The truth of the matter.
As I open the faceplate and wind the heirloom,
All it really is
– An heirloom

I notice the markings, the simple things that give life to the watch.
Little etches on the winder echo in my mind.
Each marking nothing more than
The pictures covered in brown leather and stored away,
Those images that define the nature of our being as a family.
The ultrasounds and photos of first birthdays: the mechanical gear
Movement of life
Meticulously breaking down the seconds,
And in those movements the watch draws to a conclusion.

Hearing the conductor ringing, the ticking changes to the drum of a train
In rhythm with
The exhale of the trees blowing in the wind in 1890.
With the breath of 1890 fading there will be just the watch: a family
Ticking,
Ceasing to function, exhaling a final gasp
To chime no more.

Dancing in Time

I found a city, where the endless road seemed to come to a conclusion
And a man could watch this American game
Baseball in Louisville till the sun sets on the Mighty Mississippi.
The Mississippi where a young child Samuel with a dream began to write
Those famous first words.
Water flows from north to south on the map, dividing east and west,
Taking me as logs in the load
While I write a love poem with the ferocity found
In the birth of culture, and rapids dancing in a rhythm,
Tantalizingly seductive.
My raft of wood guides me,
The flow of the journey
Stops in a bottleneck
Riots of water thick and black create falls of a place called Birmingham.
And as I float on I watch a clearing of calm water
Where men in blue ties converse with men in red ties
About how the blood of the giant dinosaurs
No longer runs thick and crude in the earth.
I wish I had met this giant rather than the men in the blue suits,
This creature of my imagination telling me this place is covered
In his body

Yet, before I think to ask him a question,
The lilies and grass of the afternoon pass on
In the wind sending me searching
For the myths of the river they call a Creek, a Cherokee,
With the language of the Iroquois in the north
Dissipating in the air.
Birds and bullfrogs call a tune in the murkiness,
Chiming in the deep corners of a grandfather's day
Louder than sounds of children with fried frog legs
Along the bank
If I listen carefully

Colorado Irish
(For Sherman Alexie)

Is it really just a passage of time
Before I too start seeing owls?
I'm just a mick of an Irishman
From where Buffalo Bill and Levi's
Scared John Wayne back into the city
Where a book called Flight began.
My professor in her red cowboy-boots
Tells me it's all postmodernism.
That seems such an inorganic way
To have a cup of coffee with
A writer called Sherman Alexie
I forget about the Big-Dipper
And think only of a horse culture
Sitting out on the Earth.

Photo from Lookout Mountain House by: Paul Deardorff

About the Author

Conor Keating was born in Boulder Colorado in 1985 after his parents Karen and Brian relocated from Michigan. He grew up in the foothills of Golden Colorado with his brother Sean, and attended Lakewood High school where he learned to love Shakespeare and public speaking. He has an avid love of fishing, skiing, tennis, swimming and spending time with his son Killian. In addition to this, he is a comic book lover of such comics as Marvel, Batman comics, and Doonesbury. He has a Peanuts collection and reads Calvin and Hobbes or watches Monty Python when trying to find balance in his life. Conor became immersed in the Punk movement as a teenager especially after attending the play Lipstick Traces in New York City. His Classic rock journey when mom gifted him a record player along with such albums as Tommy, and Houses of the Holly after screening Almost Famous. Mr. Keating attended the University of Idaho from 2003 to 2010 where he completed his degree in Creative Writing, living in the town of Moscow Idaho, where he learned to east-coast swing dance as a Swing Devil, write poetry, and became a member of Phi Kappa Tau fraternity. His poetic heroes include Tony Hoagland, Elizabeth Bishop, Billy Collins, Sharon Old's and of course the musical stylings of the Ramones. Warped is his first book.

Contributing artists

Solar Dunn:
Solar Dunn is a black, queer, digital artist based in Colorado. He is largely a character artist and graphic designer, primarily working in bright colors and semi realism such as his purple chicken based on Conor's work. After graduation with a degree in Concept Art, he aims to enter the Indie Animation workspace along with continued freelance work. He is currently open for commissions you can find him on Instagram under 'TheSolarRayy' or email him at leemikayla404@gmail.com.

Paul Deardorff:
Paul Deardorff is vice president of TKP Architects and Structural Design Partnership, in Golden CO. He's a registered architect in Colorado and Arizona and has a Bachelor of Architecture with minors in both art and interior design from the University of Idaho. Paul's designs have been published in Mountain Living, The Robb Report, LUXE, and many other design publications. Along with managing the firm, Paul specializes in space planning, architectural style development, and historical detailing. Paul enjoys hiking, biking, four-wheeling, camping, traveling, and growing orchids. He's also passionate about the design and performance of high-end sports cars. Paul's fine art varies from print, collage, etching, and now digital forms. Paul enjoys the use of intense color to create abstract imagery that stimulates emotion and visual sensation

Sean Keating:
Sean Keating is the visual counterpart to his brother Conor's literary creative expression. Inspired by Bill Plympton, John Kricfalusi, Bill Watterson, and the second golden age of comic books that coincided with his formative years he pursued a BA in Fine Arts from the University of Southern California with the goal of making a living as an illustrator. Quickly determining that a life of poverty was ill suited to his tastes, a pivot to graphic and web design serendipitously coincided with the burgeoning internet and smartphone era, allowing him to afford fancy shoes by establishing a career as a digital product designer. He still draws stupid cartoons in the little spare time he finds between raising two daughters with his long-suffering partner, Jen and managing their small hobby farm of 45(ish) animals.

Robin and Lisa Sarf:

Robin and Lisa Sarff are happily married with two wonderful children. After graduating from the University of Idaho Robin and Lisa, decided to move to the beautiful Bitterroot Valley. They have, since creating the paintings and photos used in this book, started a family and reconnected with God. Both Robin and Lisa count it a blessing to be included in the creative process of Warped and continue to be dear friends with Conor.

Publishers Note

Daxson Publishing was created to help marginalized artists and their allies publish their work, so the world can hear their voice. The vision for this publishing house is to help people get their work out there, and not have them struggle finding their way through the publishing process. Everyone's voice deserves to be heard, and we are here to help. If you are interested in submitting a manuscript, email daxsonpublishing@gmail.com. Support our cause by buying books from daxsonpublishing.com.

www.ingramcontent.com/pod-product-compliance
Lightning Source LLC
Chambersburg PA
CBHW051323120626
46547CB00015B/2373